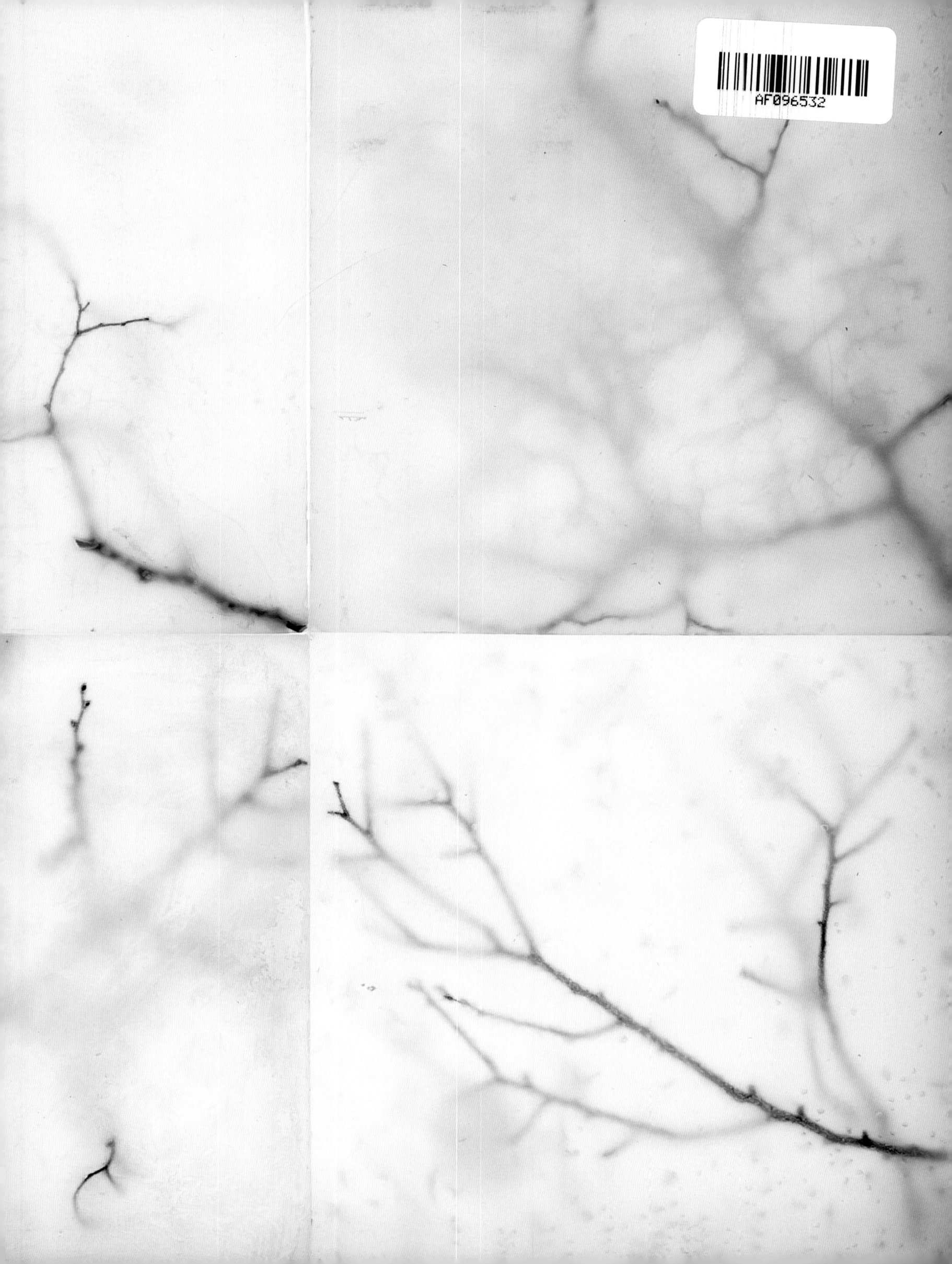

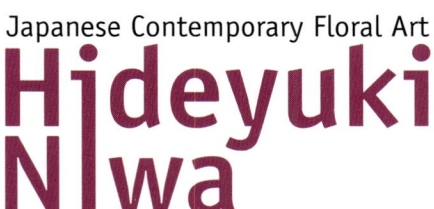

Japanese Contemporary Floral Art
Hideyuki Niwa

Eternal fragment | 永遠なる断片 | Flexigrass

Japanese Contemporary Floral Art

Hideyuki Niwa

Foreword

I'm deeply pleased with the release of Hideyuki Niwa's first book. Or maybe I should say that I'm proud of him, because I'm sure this opportunity will make him grow both as a person and as an artistic personality.

The first time I met him, Hideyuki was enrolled at a vocational school where I was a lecturer. He is the youngest of three children, with two older brothers managing their own flower shop in Aichi. As far as I know he lived in Tokyo after graduation and was employed by a flower company in that city. I also know that he won many honors in floral design competitions in Japan.

From a distance I was secretly cheering for the obedient young man that had been working so hard. At that time he contacted me asking for private lessons, from that day on Hideyuki has been my student.
When I am teaching I think all students are my equals. I don't want to make them into carbon copies of myself. I encourage them to find their own aesthetics and style. I do my best to nurture their natural talents and to make them grow. Only then students can let their personality shine through in their designs. If we can teach the next generation anything, it should be the respect for nature and the floral culture and ancient flower traditions of Japan.

Hideyuki changed little by little. His strong points are his delicate sensibility and his near perfect hand technique, as is demonstrated in this book. He impressed me with several of his works. I'm really proud of him. When he gets older and more experienced he will be a marvelous flower designer, inspiring another generation. Although he is very aware of his talent, Hideyuki never forgets to be modest about his works. When a floral designer is satisfied with his arrangements, he'll never be able to grow.

Making and publishing a book is challenging. It is a process that costs a lot of effort, energy and time and is full of nervous anticipation. After the release of the book he will feel lassitude, reflection, regret and he will be challenged to do things differently next time. Every author has to go through this cycle. The same goes for me, as Hideyuki and I, by happy coincidence, both publish a new book in 2013.

It is lonely to walk ahead of someone. But if Hideyuki will walk ahead of me one day, I'll gladly give him the necessary push in the back. I'm looking forward to that day.

Contemporary Flower Artist
Ryusaku Matsuda

丹羽英之君の仕事を讃えて

　彼の初めての作品集が発刊されることに、私は非常に喜びを感じています。かみしめている、と言った方がふさわしいかもしれません。それほど私は嬉しく思っています。これでまた私の教え子が、さらに成長していってくれるであろうと、確信しているからです。

　彼と初めて出会ったのは、私が講師をしている専門学校に彼が入学してきた時でした。彼は三人兄弟の末っ子で、二人の兄が実家のフローリストを経営しています。卒業後、彼は東京に残り、某フローリストに就職したと聞きました。また、国内での多くの大会で、優秀な成績を獲得していることも知っていました。あの大人しそうな青年が頑張っているな、と陰ながら応援していたものです。そんな彼からプライベートレッスンを受けたいと連絡が入り、その日から彼は私の教え子の一人になりました。

　私はレッスンにおいて、私と生徒は対等だと思っています。自分のコピーを作る気は全くありません。人に教えるということは、その生徒に一度身についた癖をまず確かめ、本来の資質を向上させ、生徒独自の視点で作品を創り上げさせることだと思っています。そして、日本の豊かな風土が育んだ花文化への想いを、次の世代にバトンタッチすることだとも。

　彼は少しずつ変化し、成長していきました。彼本来の持ち味である、繊細な感性と美しい手さばき、それはこの作品集にいかんなく発揮されています。私自身も刺激を受ける作品が何点もありました。これは悔しくもあり、私の誇りでもあります。年を重ね、謙虚に経験を重ねていけば、さらに味わいのある作家になっていくでしょう。作家にはもうこれで良いということは、決してありません。もし自分の作品に満足してしまったら、そこで終わりです。一生努力してください。

　一冊の作品集を出版するとは、どれほどの努力と時間と緊張感を必要とするものか。その後に感じるであろう脱力感、反省、後悔、再び次への挑戦。その繰り返しこそが、作家を成長させるのです。奇しくも、私もこの秋に作品集を上梓する予定です。同じ年に師弟そろって刊行できるとは、なんと楽しく嬉しいことでしょう。

　先を歩く者は孤独で、誰か道連れが欲しいものです。彼が私の前を歩いてくれるなら、私は喜んで彼の背中を押します。その日が来ることを心から願っています。

コンテンポラリーフラワーアーチスト
studio MATSUDA93　松田 隆作

Metamorphose

Inward #002 | うちなるもの#002 | Flexigrass | Hydrangea | Rosa | Clematis | Viburnum cilatatum | Astrantia major

8 | 9

Against | 逆らうもの | Flexigrass | Rosa

Indicatio | 気配 | Flexigrass | Rosa

Swelling up | うねり | Flexigrass | Clematis

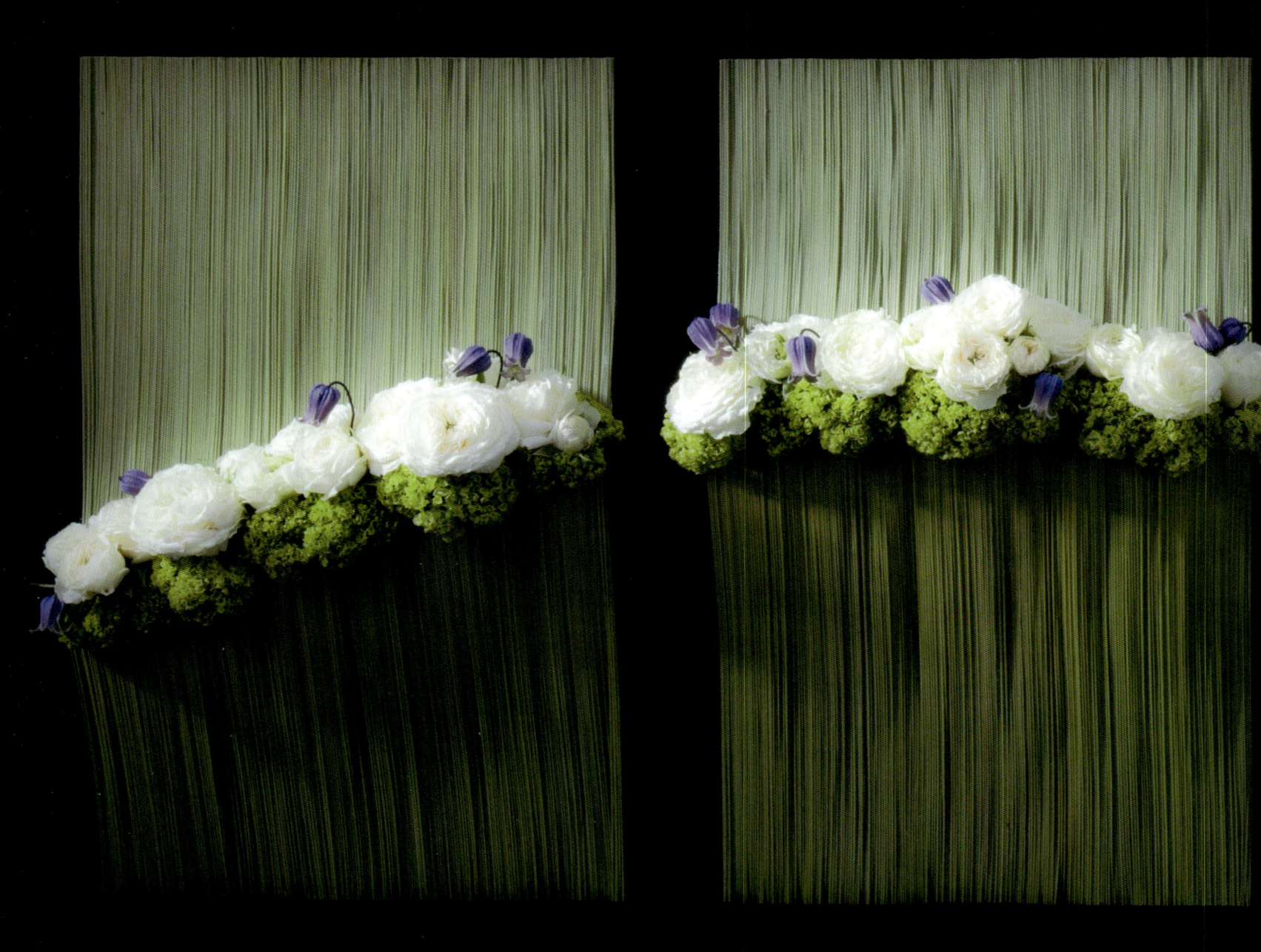

Eternal fragment | 永遠なる断片 | Flexigrass | Viburnum | Rosa | Clematis

Birth | 誕生 | Flexigrass | Dianthus barbatus L. | Rosa | Viburnum furcatum

Eternal spiral | 永遠なる螺旋 | Flexigrass

Transfiguration | 変貌 | Flexigrass

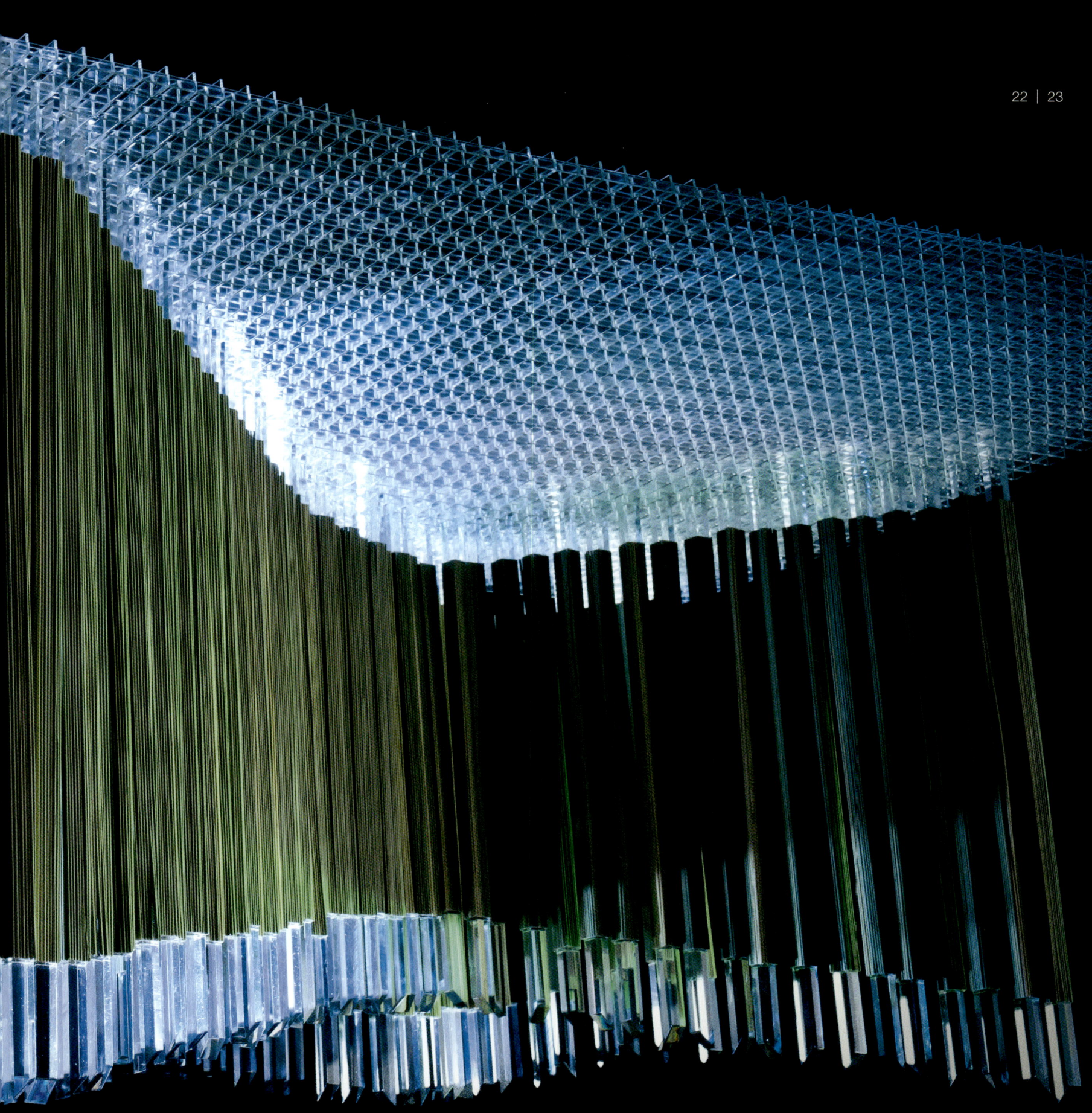

Phenomenon | 現象 | Flexigrass

Sense

Another World | もう一つの世界 | Rosa

Everlasting time #002 | 永遠なる時間 #002 | Enkianthus perulatus

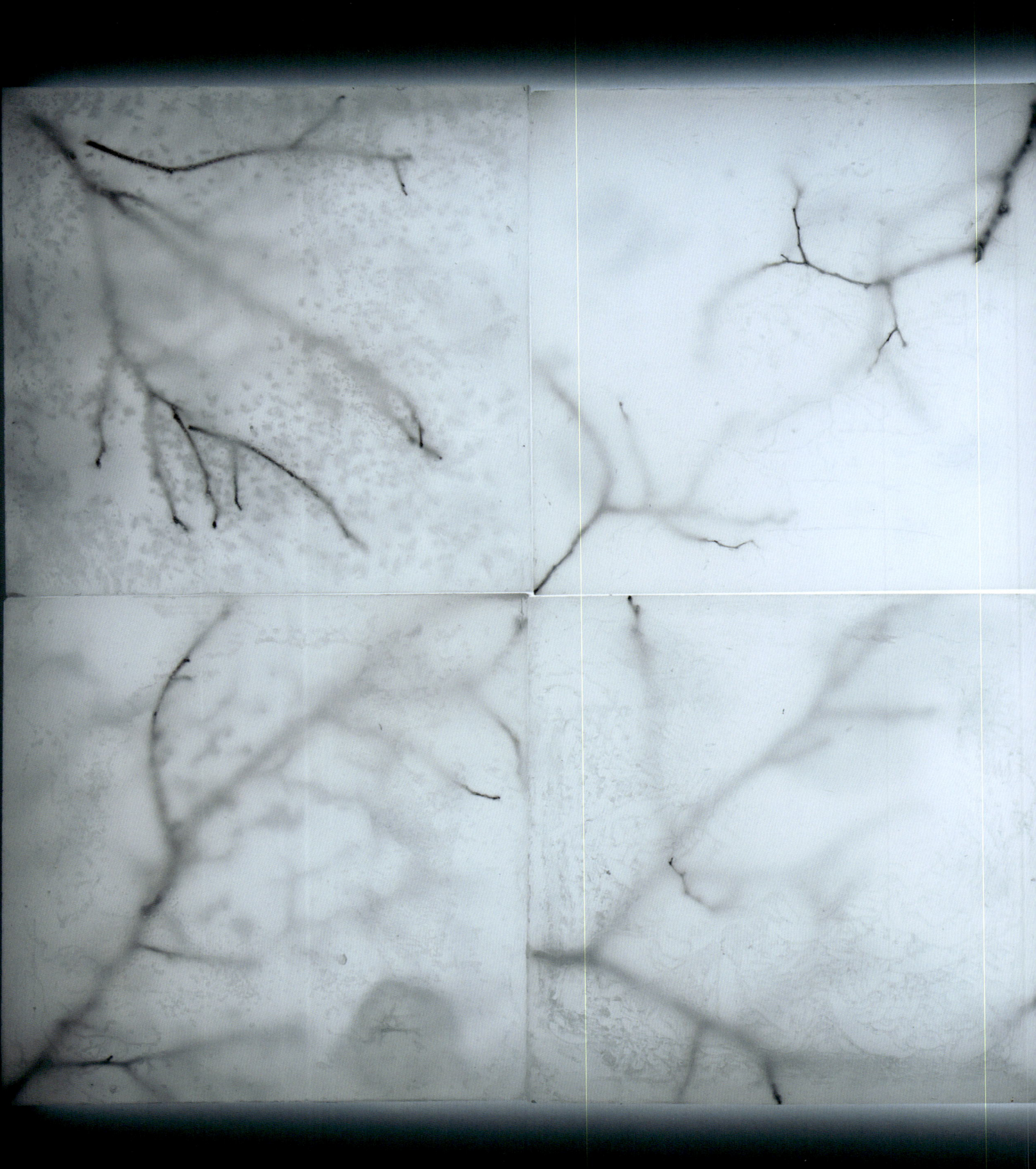

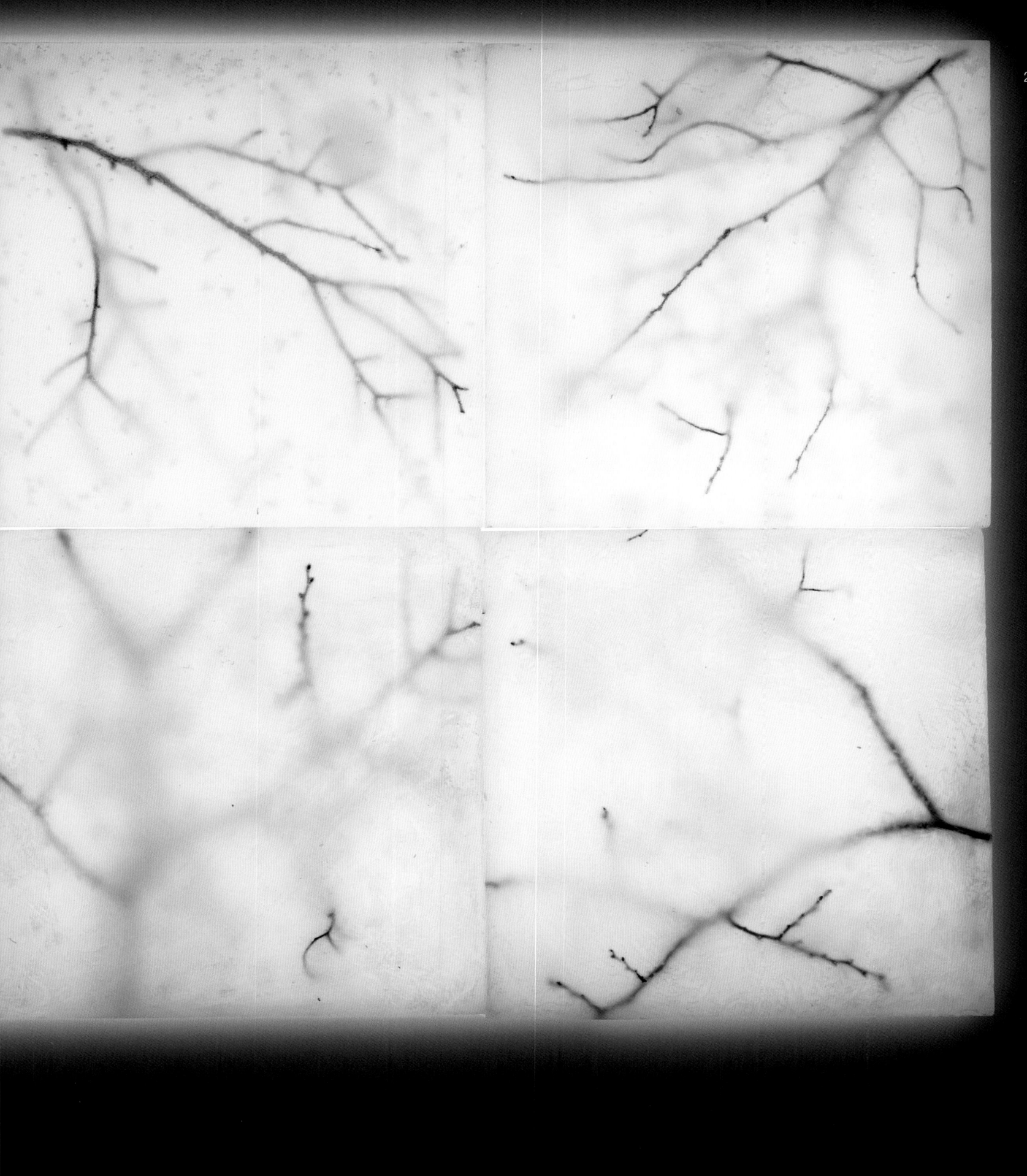

Everlasting time #007 | 永遠なる時間 #007 | Vaccinium oldhamii

Imagining and creating

Imagining and Creating, both words are deceivingly simple. But the processes of imagining and creating are less straightforward than they seem. Occasionally, I think something, an idea that I want to communicate.
I want to (re)create and share these thoughts and make them visible to other people. People often have a defined mindset of what typifies 'beauty', they have a firm definition of beauty. People's sense of beauty often defines the value they give to things. But sometimes we cannot surpass the natural beauty. Sometimes we cannot rearrange or add things to make nature more valuable or more aesthetical. Sometimes it is better not to try to emulate or imitate nature's perfection.
As flower designers we know it is impossible. Therefore we need to learn that our true mission is to create another kind of beauty with the tools that nature hands us.

想像し、創造する…

想像し、創造する… 単純であり、単純でないこの言葉に
時に私は、何かを思い、そして伝えたいと願う
人間が作り得る美の限界、そして美しさの定義とは…
基準はそれぞれが持ち、それぞれの解釈にすぎない
時に思う、自然界の生み出す芸術の美しさを
到底人間は超える事は出来ないであろう
ならば思う、超える事が出来ないのであれば、超えなくて良い
新たに創造しようと…

Feeling ｜ 感じる ｜ Iris ochroleuca ｜ Vaccinium oldhami

Atmosphere

Swaying | ゆらり | Convallaria majalis

32 | 33

Secret | 秘密 | Convallaria majalis | Viburnum

Rhythm #001 | リズム #001 | Anemone flaccida | Euonymus alatus

Rhythm #002 | リズム #002 | Anemone flaccida | Euonymus alatus

Dignified | 凛とする | Leucojum aestivum | Euonymus alatus

Dignified | 凛とする | Muscari | Euonymus alatus

Beginning | はじまり | Spiraea cantoniensis | Enkianthus perulatus

Anxiety #001 | 憂 #001 | Clematis | Enkianthus perulatus

Anxiety #002 | 憂 #002 | Euonymus alatus | Helleborus niger

Inward #003 | うちなるもの #003 | Euonymus alatus | Smilax aspera | Viburnum dilatatum

Form of interacting | 影響する形 | Dianthus barbatus L. | Rosa

Gather | 集う | Dianthus barbatus L. | Rosa

Utsuwa

Interfere | 干渉する | Pinus parviflora

Each form | **それぞれのかたち** | Dianthus barbatus L. | Rosa | Echinops ritro | Magnolia grandiflora | Enkianthus perulatus

Community | 群集 | Cucumis | Milla biflora

52 | 53

Community | 群集 | Cucumis | Clematis

Macrocosm | マクロコスモス | Phalaenopsis aphrodite | Echinops ritro

Jest | 戯れ | Clematis | Cissus

Volition | 意志 | Euonymus alatus

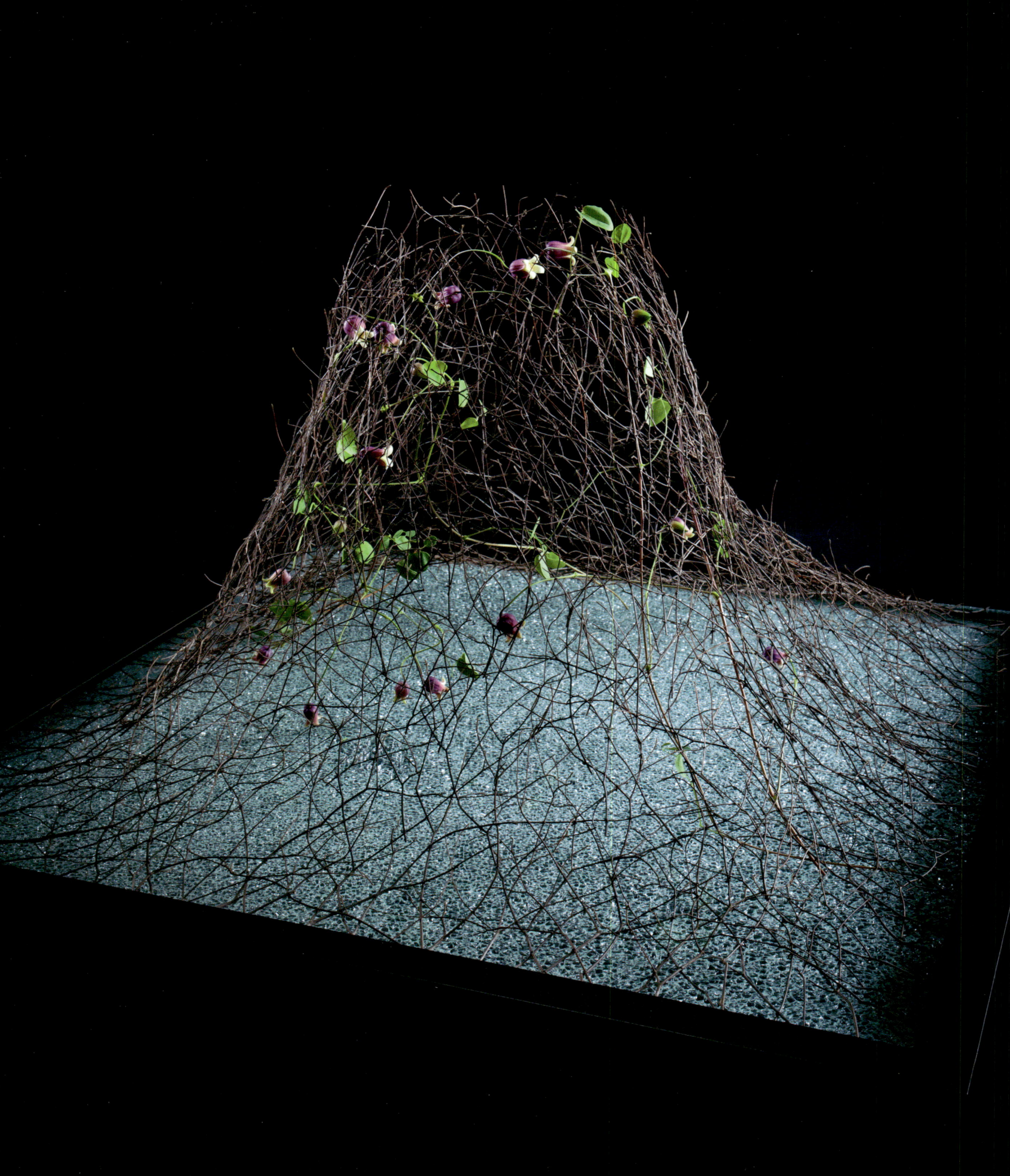

Vague #001 | 曖昧な形 #001 | Rosa | Enkianthus perulatus | Cotinus coggygria

Vague #002 | 曖昧な形 #002 | Clematis | Enkianthus perulatus

Tangled line | 絡まる線 | Allium

Tender thorn | 優しい棘 | Rosa | Leucobryum

Surface | 水面 | Cotinus coggygria | Clematis

Whirling | 渦巻くもの | Tillandsia xerographica | Echinops ritro | Phalaenopsis aphrodite

Power intersect | 交わる力 | Tillandsia xerographica

Impulse | 衝動 | Rosa

Longing | 憧憬 | Rosa | Euonymus alatus

Installation

Fairies | 妖精たち | Euonymus alatus | Clematis | Echinops ritro

A perfect fit | そこにあるもの | Euonymus alatus | Chrysanthemum

Thorn winds | 絡む棘 | Rosa | Leucobryum

Feel the wind | 風を感じて | Fosa | Hydrangea | Enkianthus perulatus

Fusion | 融合 | Pinus parviflora | Leucobryum

Successive | 連続する | Dianthus barbatus L. | Echinops ritro

Bathing | 水浴び | Dianthus barbatus L. | Clematis

Illusion | 幻影 | Rosa | Dianthus barbatus L.

Fountain of Oblivion | 忘却の泉 | Cotinus coggygria | Clematis

Harmonious | 調和 | Acer palmatum | Chrysanthemum | Leucobryum

Quietness | 静寂なる | Rosa

Beautiful flow | 美しき流れ　Elaeagnus | Clematis

The floral world is a world mirroring the human world. The life of a flower and of
a human being in essence go through the same stages: being born, growing, shining,
getting old and dying. Just as every age has its charm, all stages of the life of a flower
have beauty. Flowers can win over the heart of people, even when they are decaying.

Beauty in nature and in flowers is transient. Nature is constantly changing and
no scene can be seen twice, no tree or flower is similar. Nature has an ever changing
décor. Therein also lies the mystery and attraction of nature. All its elements are
short-lived, but it keeps repeating itself. We cannot make parts of nature ourselves,
we can only try to represent nature's mysterious beauty in a design.

In my floral works, I do like to express things. I'd like to endow my floral designs
with a lot of feeling, to make a lasting impression on people. I want them to fall in love
with the design at first sight. I give my works a heart that can attract other hearts and
make them beat a bit faster in excitement, make them happy, make them smile.

My feeling and my imagination never rest, they are aspects of my daily life that cannot
be switched off. I see design in everything around me, my heart flutters at the sight of
even the smallest, most random things. Sometimes city buildings and street life excite
me as if they were little miracles. I'm always thinking, daydreaming and inventing new
flower designs. My head never rests. It's not easy to describe the things I make, but
the inspiration can often be found in elements of daily life. Even if I notice something in
no more than a second, it catches my interest and sparks my imagination. I think the
most important thing for me is to keep an open and free mind. Not to be limited,
not to fear taboos. I'm happy that I am no slave to convention, my world is limitless.
Only in this way I'll be able to continue to create until the end of my days.

Flowers are a huge part of my daily life. I am always thinking about flowers, if that
wouldn't be the case, it would be impossible for me to use them in my work.
Flowers are life, life is important. I am really grateful for the type of work I am able to
do every day and I 'll try to keep creating the most beautiful world with flowers.

Inherit the life of flowers
Hideyuki Niwa

時に、花とは人を映す鏡であり、人の人生そのものではないかと私は考える。
人はこの世に生まれ、育ち、老い、そして死を迎える。その人生のどの場面においても、輝きを
放つ瞬間が必ずある。花も同じだ。芽吹き、育ち、蕾をつけ、咲き誇り、そして朽ち果てる。
どの瞬間も、それぞれの違った魅力で、人々を魅了して止まないのだ。朽ち果てゆくその瞬間で
さえも、花は人々の心を魅了する。

　世のすべての人々における「美」とはおそらく、花を含む「自然」が織りなすものに対して
「美しい」と思えるその感覚だろう。自然は常に変化を繰り返し、同じ光景、同じ瞬間は二度と
ない。だから人は、花の、自然の儚さを、神秘と感じるのであろう。自然のもつ神秘的な美しさ
を人の手で作り出すことなどできないとわかっていても、それでも私は自身の作品を通じて
表現したいと願う。

　私が表現したいもの。私の作品と向き合った人に、大きな感動や衝動を与えるような、心に
響く表現をしたい。作品を前に、鼓動が高まったり、胸が締めつけられたり、どこか切なかったり。
人が異性に抱く一目惚れに近い感覚を与えることができたら、とても素敵なことだと思う。

　私は常に自分の感覚を休めることをしない。作品を作るためのアンテナを立てながら日々を
暮らしている。散歩中に出会う小さな奇跡のような光景や、日常の他愛もない出来事など、
全ての要素の中にデザインの種がある。それは自然界に関するものだけに限定はしない。街並み、
建造物など、あらゆるものが対象になる。自分なりの解釈で、デザインしたり、自由に花を
活けてみたり、頭の中の空想をいつも楽しんでいる。表現したい情景は、頭を抱えて考えた
ところでそう簡単には浮かばない。日常のふとした瞬間に偶然イメージがわいてくることの方が
多い。だから、感覚を休めることができないのだ。さらに大切に思うことは、タブーを恐れず、
自由な精神を持ち続けること。何にも囚われない、制限のない世界で、自分が創りたい作品を
死ぬまで作り続けられたら、それは何て幸せなことだろう。

　自分の思考の習慣をあえて言葉にするなら、「生活を花に傾けること」。この覚悟なくして、
命ある花と真っ向から向き合うことなど到底出来ないと思い至る。まだ道半ばであるが、
花と深く関わるこの人生に感謝したい。自然界より花という命を預かりその命の力を借りて、
私が最も美しいと感じる世界を、これからも創造していきたい。

花という命を受け継ぐ者として
丹羽英之

Profile

Hideyuki Niwa was born in 1973 in Aichi. At the age of 20 he graduated from Tokyo's flower college and in the same year he got employed by Kamon Flower Gate Co Ltd; a fruitful environment for an artist eager to learn and develop.

Hideyuki Niwa was manager and chief floral designer of FLORÉAL OPAQUE Marunouchi, a company organizing wedding ceremonies at hotels in Japan and abroad. He starts his own design team 'Hideyuki Niwa Design Office' in 2013. He often takes part in competitions to challenge himself and tries creating and photographing a new design every day to get a thorough understanding of the characteristics of flowers and their possibilities. Hideyuki teams up with his brother Sinji in his quest to create a new sort of flower design - combining flowers with other materials to bring the designs and floral arrangements to the next level, hence the name of their partnership 'mixture'.

Most important realisations and exhibitions
2002	Selection of flower arrangements for the Flower Exposition of Kanto Tokai Prize of Minister of Agriculture
2004-2007	Designs and demonstration at International Rose and Gardening show
2005-2007	Exhibtion of works and demonstration at the International flower EXPO
2007	Fifth place in the JFTD Japan Cup
2009	Floral designs for wedding ceremony and room decoration at 'AYANA Resort and Spa BARI'
2009	Seventh place in the JFTD Japan Cup
2010	Bronze Leaf award in the 'International Floral Art 10/11' (Belgium) Fourth place in the JFTD Japan Cup
2012	Gold Leaf (first prize) in the 'International Floral Art 12/13' (Belgium) Second place in the JFTD Japan Cup Solo Exhibition 'Hideyuki NIWA Contemporary Floral Art' in Tokyo

丹羽英之　Hideyuki Niwa | 1973

愛知県生まれ。1993年、株式会社花門フラワーゲート入社。
FLORÉALオペーク丸の内店マネージャー・チーフデザイナーを経て、
2013年、自身のデザインチームHideyuki Niwa Design Officeを立ち上げる。
国内外のホテル・式場のウェディングのプロデュースを始め、有名ショップのショールームやレストラン等のコーディネートを担当する。
「混合・融合」をテーマに、植物と異素材を組み合われることにより新しい価値観を追求する
フラワーパフォーマンスユニット「mixture」を兄である丹羽伸次と結成。独自の世界観を表現する
フラワーパフォーマンスを各地で行う。

【主な経歴】
2002	関東東海花の博覧会　アレンジ部門にて金賞・農林水産大臣賞受賞
2004-2007	国際バラとガーデニングショーにてデザインワークとデモンストレーション
2005-2007	国際フラワーEXPO(IFEX)にてデザインワークとデモンストレーション
2007	一般社団法人日本生花通信配達協会主催 ジャパンカップ2007にて5位入賞
2009	「AYANA Resort Spa BARI」のウエディングフラワー及び館内装花をプロデュース 一般社団法人日本生花通信配達協会主催 ジャパンカップ2009にて7位入賞
2010	ベルギー【International Floral Art 10/11】にてブロンズリーフ賞受賞 一般社団法人日本生花通信配達協会主催 ジャパンカップ2010にて4位入賞
2012	ベルギー【International Floral Art 12/13】にて最優秀賞ゴールドリーフ賞受賞 一般社団法人日本生花通信配達協会主催 ジャパンカップ2012にて準優勝 東京丸の内にて初の単独個展「Hideyuki NIWA Contemporary Floral Art」を開催

Creations / Text | フラワーデザイン / 文章
Hideyuki Niwa | 丹羽 英之

Assistant | アシスタント
Chika Tsukada | 塚田 知佳

Photography | 撮影
Kiyokazu Nakajima | 中島 清一

Translation | 翻訳
Yayoi Noguchi | 野口 弥生

Cooperator | 協力
Noriko Ogawa | 小川 典子

Sponsor of photography | 撮影協力
FLORÉAL
mixture NW-Blood Design unit
Museum of Contemporary Art Tokyo | 東京都現代美術館

Recommendation | 推薦文
Ryusaku Matsuda | 松田 隆作
studio MATSUDA93

Sponsor of materials | 花材協力
Plants Partner Co, Ltd | 株式会社プランツパートナー
2-2-1 Tokai Ota-ku Tokyo Japan | 東京都大田区東海2-2-1
Tel +81 3-5492-4191
Fax +81 3-5492-4194
http://www.plantspartner.co.jp

Ichikawa Rose garden Co, Ltd | 有限会社市川バラ園
37-2 Tamagawa Mishima-City Shizuoka Japan | 静岡県三島市玉川37-2
Tel +81 55-975-9141
Fax +81 55-975-9148
http://www.ichikawa-baraen.com

Support | 後援
Hanasei Co, Ltd | 株式会社花成
3-14-8 Hirashiba-cho Toyota-City Aichi Japan | 愛知県豊田市平芝町3-14-8
Tel +81 565-32-3096
Fax +81 565-34-3621
http://www.hanasei-inc.jp

Special Support | 特別協力
Kamon Flowergate Co, Ltd | 株式会社花門フラワーゲート
3-19-2 Hachobori Chuo-ku Tokyo Japan | 東京都中央区八丁堀3-19-2
Tel +81 3-5541-4187
Fax +81 3-3523-8801
http://www.flowergate.co.jp

Final Editing | 編集
Katrien Van Moerbeke

Print | 印刷
PurePrint
www.pureprint.be

Lay-out | レイアウト
Group Van Damme
www.groupvandamme.eu

Published by | 発行
Stichting Kunstboek bvba
Legeweg 165
B-8020 Oostkamp
Belgium
Tel. +32 50 46 19 10
Fax + 32 50 46 19 18
info@stichtingkunstboek.com
www.stichtingkunstboek.com

ISBN 978-90-5856-437-5
D/2013/6407/7
NUR 421

All rights reserved. No part of this publication may be reproduced, stored in a database or in a retrieval system, or transmitted in any form or by any means, electronically, mechanically, by print, microfilm or otherwise without prior permission from the Publisher.

© Stichting Kunstboek 2013